THE Intuition BUILDER

SIGNS, SIGNALS & SYNCHRONICITIES

Connect with your Spirit Team to
Co-Create an Easeful & Prosperous
Life of Impact & Soul Fulfillment

GUIDE + WORKBOOK

DISCLAIMER

All the information, techniques, skills and concepts contained within this publication are of the nature of general comment only and are not in any way recommended as individual advice. The intent is to offer a variety of information to provide a wider range of choices now and in the future, recognising that we all have widely diverse circumstances and viewpoints. Should any reader choose to make use of the information contained herein, this is their decision, and the contributors (and their companies), authors and publishers do not assume any responsibilities whatsoever under any condition or circumstances. It is recommended the reader obtain their own independent advice.

Copyright © 2020 by Julie Lewin & Tash Lewin

All rights reserved. No part of this publication may be reproduced, stored in a retrieval system, or transmitted in any form or by any means, electronic mechanical, photocopying, recording or otherwise, without the prior written permission from the publisher.

All graphic design & typesetting by: Tash Lewin

National Library of Australia

Cataloguing-in-Publication entry:

Lewin, Julie, 1959-

Lewin, Tash, 1984-

The Intuition Builder: Signs, Signals & Synchronicities / Julie Lewin & Tash Lewin

1st ed.

ISBN: 978-0-9874957-7-8

1. Intuition. 2. Entrepreneurship. 3. Spirituality. 4. Self-Help. 5. Meditation.

Published by Celestial Consciousness Publishing

PO Box 1142, Milton BC Qld 4064

Email: support@lightcodelab.com

Phone: +61 421 542 436

For those who believe in magic

Have you taken our free QUIZ to determine your
Dominant Intuitive Language?

TAKE IT NOW
lightcodelab.com/quiz

Contents

05
WELCOME MESSAGE

06
HOW TO USE THIS BOOK

07
CLAIRVOYANCE

45
CLAIRAUDIENCE

90
CLAIRSENTIENCE

128
CLAIRALIENCE

159
CLAIRCOGNIZANCE

198
TALLY SHEETS

05

Welcome
my friend

Thank you for purchasing "The Intuition Builder: Signs, Signals & Synchronicities" Guide + Workbook. We are so excited for you to learn more about your Intuitive Languages and how you can integrate them into your day to day life and business.

We are all about incorporating practical spirituality, lived in a grounded way, into our life & business. Creating an extraordinary ordinary life you don't want to escape from. Learning about yourself, and how you naturally live and grow in the world is essential for bringing your message and soul work to the world.

You have come here again, to physical life, for reasons your Soul knows, and we are grateful that we can be a small part of how you uncover your answers. When you connect with your Spirit Team (Guides, Higher Self, Creative Muse, Angels, or even Ascended Masters) in the Subtle Realm, you unlock a support system that will guide you on your journey of self-discovery, spiritual development, and business entrepreneurship.

Let's get you connected!

Blessings,

Julie & Tash Lewin

Mother-Daughter Duo

HOW TO USE THIS GUIDE

STEPS TO TAKE

01
CHECK IN WITH YOU

As with any external wisdom you seek, you must first go within, to determine if it resonates with you and your own intuition.

This is information we have downloaded and formed into a system to access my own Intuition, but that doesn't mean it will be right for you. As always, take what resonates and integrate it, and leave what doesn't.

Also, with any quiz you take to learn more about yourself, your results will be dependent on what you consciously know in that moment. For example if you have been using an Intuitive Language consciously, then you may be more likely to remember these signs while doing the quiz. As you use this book, be open to receiving all of the signs you are given to determine your Dominant Language.

02
TAKE NOTE

As you begin to access these Intuition Languages consciously, you may start to notice that you are getting other signs that are different to the Dominant type you received in this quiz. By taking note of these, you can determine whether you actually access a different Dominant Intuitive Language or if you are simply using multiple languages for different purposes.

We are able to access all of the Intuitive Languages, however it is beneficial to really hone your Dominant Language so you are getting consistent signs, signals and guidance.

As you get consistent with your Dominant Language, you can begin to consciously access all of your Clair's.

03
TRACK YOUR SIGNS

By tracking what signs & signals you receive, you can begin to see a pattern of when and where you receive them.

For example, you may get visual signs when you are receiving confirmations for yourself, but you may access Clairsentient physical signs when you are working with clients or downloading intuitive notes for others.

By tracking when and where these differences occur, you can begin to more consciously access and request guidance from your Spirit Team.

YOUR INTUITIVE LANGUAGE GUIDE

Your Dominant Intuitive Language is:

Clairvoyance

CLEAR SEEING

> "I shut my eyes in order to see."
>
> – Paul Gauguin

Your Dominant Intuitive Language is:
Clairvoyance
CLEAR SEEING

You are a visionary. You see what is, has been and can be in the future. You work with the Subtle Realm, pulling visions of what could be into the now, so that others can work with them. Without you there would be no art, beauty, form. You see the threads that connect everything within the Matrix and you pull it out of the ether and make it manifest.

You have the extraordinary ability to receive intuitive impressions visually, in the form of symbols, images, colours and visions. These may be physical in the world around you or in the mind's eye. They may be detailed or a flash of impressions. You may receive these visions while awake, in meditation, dreaming or in a lucid dream state.

The key differentiator for this Language type is that you SEE things.

You use language like "Ah, yes, I see", "I've had a vision", "I had a flash of", "See, I told you so", "I see what you mean"

To hone this ability and use it consciously during your co-creating work, continue reading.

10

Common Signs & Signals

REPEATING NUMBERS i.e. 1111, 333, 444, 777, 999, 123, 345, 0088, etc : These are known as Angel Numbers, and there are channelled meanings and symbolism for these number sequences available http://sacredscribesangel-numbers.blogspot.com/p/index-numbers.html. So if you begin seeing these numbers repeat, you can either look up the number sequence and determine if the meaning resonates, or simply use the fact that numbers are repeating as a confirmation for what you have asked or what you are thinking about.

TOTEM ANIMALS : You may see animals in the physical world, or within visions, dreams or meditation. This https://www.spiritanimal.info/ provides meanings & symbolism for different totem animals. By requesting confirmation from your Spirit Team, you can determine if an animal is with you as a Spirit Guide with it's powers available to you, or if you are to use the animal symbolism as confirmation for a choice or path you are on.

For example, the fly has symbolism of quick and abrupt changes within all aspects of your life and that if you move quickly, you will have access to exponentially growing sources of abundance. So, if you have been questioning the direction of your business, or perhaps you are launching a new product and you are unsure if now is the right time, and then you start seeing a lot of flies around you, you can take this as a positive confirmation, that yes, the time is right for this move and that you should act quickly.

Now, if the Fly was your Spirit Animal, then you might see this as providing you with the Ability to move quickly, act decisively and attract abundance into your business.

Photo by: Carlos Irineu da Costa on Unsplash

Photo by: Ilinca Roman on Unsplash

SEEING IMAGERY IN THE WORLD AROUND YOU: Have you ever asked a question or thought of something you desire and then you start seeing it everywhere? Or you start seeing the same object or thing everywhere you go?

For example, a friend of mine started seeing red cars everywhere she went. She was trying to decide if she should start a new project, even though she was meant to be taking a break from business. In her search for the meaning behind the red cars, she contacted Julie Lewin for her interpretation.

"The car could mean setting wheels in motion, that a car gets you to a destination that you want to go. Red is a symbol for passion or excitement." So she was seeing that something she was passionate about would lead her to set wheels in motion and get her moving forward. BUT all the cars were always parked, and we deduced that this was because she still had some decisions to make that would determine when she turned the car on and started moving. As soon as she realised this, and figured out what she needed to know, she started seeing red cars driving everywhere she went. Then she saw a red car drive through a red light, and knew that she needed to slow down and take it one leg of the journey at a time, not try and rush forward.

REPEATING DREAM SYMBOLISM: Dream symbolism is available through a variety of websites and if you are experiencing similar events or seeing similar patterns in your dreams/meditations then you may want to look up some of the common interpretations. Be aware that there are many variations of these interpretations, and if one doesn't resonate with you, then find one that does. Also be aware of all of the elements of the dream sequence, as they will be communicating as a whole rather than individual symbols.

For example, if in your dream/vision you have your car stolen, it might indicate a lack of control over where you are going and how you are getting there; but, if you had your wallet in the car, then you could also be concerned about how you are going to pay to get where you are going or where the money you need is coming from. Now, if there is a lion standing beside you, then you may be required to gather your courage before stepping forward. If an alternative mode of transport is in place of your car, then you may need to be flexible about how you get to your destination.

What to do when you are stuck

When you find yourself feeling overwhelmed, panicked, frustrated, angry, sad, hopeless, drowning... take a deep breath, and go somewhere where you can sit quietly.

The first thing you can do, is simply breathe; take a deep breath in for 5 counts, hold for 5 counts, and then breathe out for 5 counts, for 5 minutes.

When you are in this emotive space, it can be hard to access your intuition clearly. You need to get your body out of it's fight or flight response in order to see what you need to see to move forward.

Once you are feeling calmer, close your eyes and go within. You have access to your Spirit Team, who are ready and willing to assist you in any way you need, but you have to ask them. This is the key. They are causal beings and are not able to directly affect the physical realm. So in order to get the inspiration, guidance, answers, feedback, etc that you require to make a decision, you must ask. When you ask for guidance, you need to look for the answers in a way that aligns with your Dominant Intuitive Language. If you want help with connecting to your Spirit Team, purchase our Meet Your Muse Meditation bundle https://lightcodelab.com/meetyourmuse). You may receive guidance in this space, or if you are out in the world, they may be physical/metaphysical signs.

Refer back to the previous pages where we explored these signs in more detail.

- Animals
- Repeating numbers
- Visions in your minds eye
- Events occuring around you
- Seeing repeating objects or images

Seek these signs while asking questions of your Spirit Team. If you need to make a decision, ask "which option is for my highest good" or "give me a sign for what I need to do next to stay in flow and be on my path".

All choices will eventually lead you where you need to go, however, some may be quicker than others. Start to seek the signs that show you when you are in flow and when you are out of flow. If you can't understand the signs, join us in the Facebook group: MAGIC NOT LOGIC with Julie & Tash Lewin, where we assist with Decoding Signs & Signals. The more you practice, the easier and quicker you will interpret what is being shown.

How do you make the picture clearer?

When you start out, it can be difficult to know whether you are just imagining what you are seeing or if it is really coming from the Universe. Knowing when you are connected in will be different for everyone, and so you will need to seek a confirmation that is unique to you.

If you see a visual sign, either in your mind's eye or in the world, and you're not sure if it means anything, ask your Spirit Team to adjust the antenna as it were (this shows my age, as I remember a time when you used to have to adjust the bunny ear antenna to make the tv clearer and less fuzzy lol). So if your vision is fuzzy, simply ask for them to boost the signal and make it clearer for you.

You might ask them to show you the same sign multiple times, if you want to be sure it is one. Or you may ask for the sign to be brighter than everything else, like with a glow around it. If you only get visions in a flash which are too quick for you, ask them to slow down the visions so you have more time to interpret them. If the symbolism (because that is how the Universe communicates) is too vague for you to understand, ask to be guided to resources that can help you interpret the symbols.

Like anything, accessing and using your Intuition in your business and daily life takes practice. You are learning a new language and like any new language, the integration into your vocabulary takes time. Be patient with yourself, and seek interpretation decoding in our free Facebook group **MAGIC NOT LOGIC with Julie & Tash Lewin.**

INTUITIVE LANGUAGE WORKSHEETS

Signs & Signals Tracking Sheets for

Clairvoyance

CLEAR SEEING

REPEATING NUMBERS

What numbers did you see repeating?

EXAMPLES:
111's, 222's, 333's, 444's, 555's, 666's, 777's, 888's, 999's, 000's, 1234...9, 0101.

What were you thinking about, contemplating or asking for guidance on when these occurred?

What revelations did you have when reflecting on the symbolism of these numbers?

SEEING ANIMALS

What animals did you see repeating?

EXAMPLES:
Crow, butterfly, dragonfly, fly, beetle, ant, dog, cat, tiger, lion, bird, chicken, wolf, otter, bear, bat, dolphin, eagle, fox, dragon, horse, cow, frog, owl, rabbit, spider, swan, turtle, whale...

What were you thinking about, contemplating or asking for guidance on when these occurred?

What revelations did you have when reflecting on the symbolism of these animals?

REPEATING DREAM SYMBOLISM

What did you see in your dreams/visions?

EXAMPLES:
Running late, losing something, meeting/losing someone, finding money, dying, running, flying, jumping, driving, missing transport...

What were you thinking about, contemplating or asking for guidance on before these occurred?

What revelations did you have when reflecting on the symbolism of these dreams/visions?

REPEATING IMAGERY

What objects, places, images did you repeatedly see?

EXAMPLES:
Red cars, clocks, beaches, snow, mountains, cities, money, bells, lightbulb, colours, book covers, appliances, paintings, devices, old style objects...

What were you thinking about, contemplating or asking for guidance on before/when these occurred?

What revelations did you have when reflecting on the symbolism of repeating objects, places, and images?

REPEATING NUMBERS

What numbers did you see repeating?

EXAMPLES:
111's, 222's, 333's, 444's, 555's, 666's, 777's, 888's, 999's, 000's, 1234...9, 0101.

What were you thinking about, contemplating or asking for guidance on when these occurred?

What revelations did you have when reflecting on the symbolism of these numbers?

SEEING ANIMALS

What animals did you see repeating?

EXAMPLES:
Crow, butterfly, dragonfly, fly, beetle, ant, dog, cat, tiger, lion, bird, chicken, wolf, otter, bear, bat, dolphin, eagle, fox, dragon, horse, cow, frog, owl, rabbit, spider, swan, turtle, whale...

What were you thinking about, contemplating or asking for guidance on when these occurred?

What revelations did you have when reflecting on the symbolism of these animals?

REPEATING DREAM SYMBOLISM

What did you see in your dreams/visions?

EXAMPLES:
Running late, losing something, meeting/losing someone, finding money, dying, running, flying, jumping, driving, missing transport...

What were you thinking about, contemplating or asking for guidance on before these occurred?

What revelations did you have when reflecting on the symbolism of these dreams/visions?

REPEATING IMAGERY

What objects, places, images did you repeatedly see?

EXAMPLES:
Red cars, clocks, beaches, snow, mountains, cities, money, bells, lightbulb, colours, book covers, appliances, paintings, devices, old style objects...

What were you thinking about, contemplating or asking for guidance on before/when these occurred?

What revelations did you have when reflecting on the symbolism of repeating objects, places, and images?

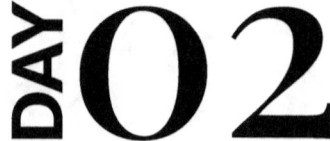

REPEATING NUMBERS

What numbers did you see repeating?

EXAMPLES:
111's, 222's, 333's, 444's, 555's, 666's, 777's, 888's, 999's, 000's, 1234...9, 0101.

What were you thinking about, contemplating or asking for guidance on when these occurred?

What revelations did you have when reflecting on the symbolism of these numbers?

SEEING ANIMALS

What animals did you see repeating?

EXAMPLES:
Crow, butterfly, dragonfly, fly, beetle, ant, dog, cat, tiger, lion, bird, chicken, wolf, otter, bear, bat, dolphin, eagle, fox, dragon, horse, cow, frog, owl, rabbit, spider, swan, turtle, whale...

What were you thinking about, contemplating or asking for guidance on when these occurred?

What revelations did you have when reflecting on the symbolism of these animals?

REPEATING DREAM SYMBOLISM

What did you see in your dreams/visions?

EXAMPLES:
Running late, losing something, meeting/losing someone, finding money, dying, running, flying, jumping, driving, missing transport...

What were you thinking about, contemplating or asking for guidance on before these occurred?

What revelations did you have when reflecting on the symbolism of these dreams/visions?

REPEATING IMAGERY

What objects, places, images did you repeatedly see?

EXAMPLES:
Red cars, clocks, beaches, snow, mountains, cities, money, bells, lightbulb, colours, book covers, appliances, paintings, devices, old style objects...

What were you thinking about, contemplating or asking for guidance on before/when these occurred?

What revelations did you have when reflecting on the symbolism of repeating objects, places, and images?

REPEATING NUMBERS

What numbers did you see repeating?

EXAMPLES:
111's, 222's, 333's,
444's, 555's, 666's,
777's, 888's, 999's,
000's, 1234...9,
0101.

What were you thinking about, contemplating or asking for guidance on when these occurred?

What revelations did you have when reflecting on the symbolism of these numbers?

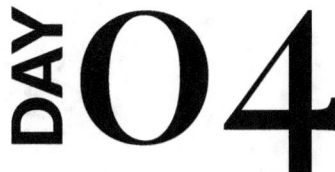

SEEING ANIMALS

What animals did you see repeating?

EXAMPLES:
Crow, butterfly, dragonfly, fly, beetle, ant, dog, cat, tiger, lion, bird, chicken, wolf, otter, bear, bat, dolphin, eagle, fox, dragon, horse, cow, frog, owl, rabbit, spider, swan, turtle, whale...

What were you thinking about, contemplating or asking for guidance on when these occurred?

What revelations did you have when reflecting on the symbolism of these animals?

REPEATING DREAM SYMBOLISM

What did you see in your dreams/visions?

EXAMPLES:
Running late, losing something, meeting/losing someone, finding money, dying, running, flying, jumping, driving, missing transport...

What were you thinking about, contemplating or asking for guidance on before these occurred?

What revelations did you have when reflecting on the symbolism of these dreams/visions?

REPEATING IMAGERY

What objects, places, images did you repeatedly see?

EXAMPLES:
Red cars, clocks, beaches, snow, mountains, cities, money, bells, lightbulb, colours, book covers, appliances, paintings, devices, old style objects...

What were you thinking about, contemplating or asking for guidance on before/when these occurred?

What revelations did you have when reflecting on the symbolism of repeating objects, places, and images?

REPEATING NUMBERS

What numbers did you see repeating?

EXAMPLES:
111's, 222's, 333's, 444's, 555's, 666's, 777's, 888's, 999's, 000's, 1234...9, 0101.

What were you thinking about, contemplating or asking for guidance on when these occurred?

What revelations did you have when reflecting on the symbolism of these numbers?

SEEING ANIMALS

What animals did you see repeating?

| EXAMPLES:
| Crow, butterfly, dragonfly, fly, beetle, ant, dog, cat, tiger, lion, bird, chicken, wolf, otter, bear, bat, dolphin, eagle, fox, dragon, horse, cow, frog, owl, rabbit, spider, swan, turtle, whale...

What were you thinking about, contemplating or asking for guidance on when these occurred?

What revelations did you have when reflecting on the symbolism of these animals?

REPEATING DREAM SYMBOLISM

What did you see in your dreams/visions?

EXAMPLES:
Running late, losing something, meeting/losing someone, finding money, dying, running, flying, jumping, driving, missing transport...

What were you thinking about, contemplating or asking for guidance on before these occurred?

What revelations did you have when reflecting on the symbolism of these dreams/visions?

REPEATING IMAGERY

What objects, places, images did you repeatedly see?

EXAMPLES:
Red cars, clocks, beaches, snow, mountains, cities, money, bells, lightbulb, colours, book covers, appliances, paintings, devices, old style objects...

What were you thinking about, contemplating or asking for guidance on before/when these occurred?

What revelations did you have when reflecting on the symbolism of repeating objects, places, and images?

REPEATING NUMBERS

What numbers did you see repeating?

EXAMPLES:
111's, 222's, 333's, 444's, 555's, 666's, 777's, 888's, 999's, 000's, 1234...9, 0101.

What were you thinking about, contemplating or asking for guidance on when these occurred?

What revelations did you have when reflecting on the symbolism of these numbers?

SEEING ANIMALS

What animals did you see repeating?

EXAMPLES:
Crow, butterfly, dragonfly, fly, beetle, ant, dog, cat, tiger, lion, bird, chicken, wolf, otter, bear, bat, dolphin, eagle, fox, dragon, horse, cow, frog, owl, rabbit, spider, swan, turtle, whale...

What were you thinking about, contemplating or asking for guidance on when these occurred?

What revelations did you have when reflecting on the symbolism of these animals?

REPEATING DREAM SYMBOLISM

What did you see in your dreams/visions?

EXAMPLES:
Running late, losing something, meeting/losing someone, finding money, dying, running, flying, jumping, driving, missing transport...

What were you thinking about, contemplating or asking for guidance on before these occurred?

What revelations did you have when reflecting on the symbolism of these dreams/visions?

REPEATING IMAGERY

What objects, places, images did you repeatedly see?

EXAMPLES:
Red cars, clocks, beaches, snow, mountains, cities, money, bells, lightbulb, colours, book covers, appliances, paintings, devices, old style objects...

What were you thinking about, contemplating or asking for guidance on before/when these occurred?

What revelations did you have when reflecting on the symbolism of repeating objects, places, and images?

REPEATING NUMBERS

What numbers did you see repeating?

EXAMPLES:
111's, 222's, 333's, 444's, 555's, 666's, 777's, 888's, 999's, 000's, 1234...9, 0101.

What were you thinking about, contemplating or asking for guidance on when these occurred?

What revelations did you have when reflecting on the symbolism of these numbers?

SEEING ANIMALS

What animals did you see repeating?

EXAMPLES:
Crow, butterfly, dragonfly, fly, beetle, ant, dog, cat, tiger, lion, bird, chicken, wolf, otter, bear, bat, dolphin, eagle, fox, dragon, horse, cow, frog, owl, rabbit, spider, swan, turtle, whale...

What were you thinking about, contemplating or asking for guidance on when these occurred?

What revelations did you have when reflecting on the symbolism of these animals?

REPEATING DREAM SYMBOLISM

What did you see in your dreams/visions?

EXAMPLES:
Running late, losing something, meeting/losing someone, finding money, dying, running, flying, jumping, driving, missing transport...

What were you thinking about, contemplating or asking for guidance on before these occurred?

What revelations did you have when reflecting on the symbolism of these dreams/visions?

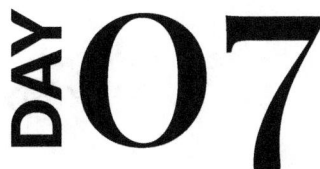

REPEATING IMAGERY

What objects, places, images did you repeatedly see?

EXAMPLES:
Red cars, clocks, beaches, snow, mountains, cities, money, bells, lightbulb, colours, book covers, appliances, paintings, devices, old style objects...

What were you thinking about, contemplating or asking for guidance on before/when these occurred?

What revelations did you have when reflecting on the symbolism of repeating objects, places, and images?

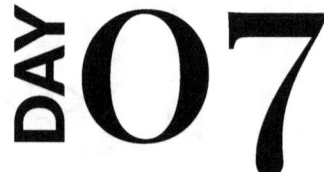

REFLECTION TIME

What did you discover about your Dominant Intuitive Language?

What signs & signals did you experience most often?

Did you access any of the other Dominant Intuitive Languages?

ACTIVITIES TO ENHANCE YOUR CONNECTION

When doing any tasks or activities where you are connecting with your Intuition, ask yourself: "What am I seeing physically and psychically?"

TAKE PHOTOS OF SMALL THINGS ON A MICRO LEVEL

1. Find a flower or object that catches your eye
2. Zoom in using your phone or camera
3. Focus the lens so that the image is clear
4. Still your breath and energy
5. Take the photo without moving the camera

SACRED ART COLLAGE

1. Get some magazines or brochures
2. Focus and connect with your Spirit Team
3. Flick through the magazines without conscious thought
4. Collect pictures that jump out or glow in some way
5. Rip or cut around the individual images you want to use
6. Place the images (without glueing) on a piece of paper/card
7. Once they are in place in a way that makes the whole piece pop, glue the images down

NATURE MANDALA

1. Go for a walk out in nature near you
2. Scan your environment as you walk
3. As objects jump out, pick them up and place them in a bag
4. When you stop seeing things pop out at you, take your collection home
5. Sort your collection on a table
6. Begin laying your objects out on a piece of paper, card or art board
7. Take a photo of it from above

We will be running online classes on all of the above, so keep an eye on our website and social media for updates.

YOUR INTUITIVE LANGUAGE GUIDE

Your Dominant Intuitive Language is:

Clairaudience

CLEAR HEARING

> "The quieter you become, the more you are able to hear."
>
> – Rumi

Your Dominant Intuitive Language is:
Clairaudience
CLEAR HEARING

You are a maestro and virtuoso of the spirit world. You hear what is said, and that which is left unsaid. You hear the music of the spheres, and the commands of your soul. You bring to life that which others can't hear, and you bring magic to life. The world needs you to listen, with all your heart, and speak with the power of truth and love.

You have the extraordinary ability to receive intuitive impressions through sound, in the form of songs, spoken words, sound effects and music. These may be physical in the world around you or psychically perceived. They may be whole conversations or fleeting instructions. You may receive these words of wisdom while awake, in meditation, dreaming or in a lucid dream state.

The key differentiator for this Language type is that you HEAR things.

You use language like "Did you hear that?", "Yes, I was told", "I heard a voice say", "That's what I heard", "I hear you"

To hone this ability and use it consciously during your co-creating work, continue reading.

48

Common Signs & Signals

ALARMS, HORNS, SIRENS, BELLS: When you hear these sound effects, stop, recall what you were thinking, saying or doing when you heard them. This is the Universe saying take note.

For example, I was sitting with a friend of mine and we were discussing whether to make a choice in our shared business. From outside we heard a car screech to a halt right outside her house. I looked at her and said "we need to put on the brakes, and really think about this before we make a decision.

VERBAL INSTRUCTIONS: These can be out loud, outside of youself or they can be inside your mind. It can feel like it is going in one ear, moving through, and going out the other ear. It can feel as though it disappears as soon as it touches your conscious mind if you don't catch it in time.

For example, as Ruth Stone (American Poet) was growing up in rural Virginia, she would be out, working in the fields and she would feel and hear a poem coming at her from over the landscape. It was like a thunderous train of air and it would come barrelling down at her over the landscape. And when she felt it coming . . . 'cause it would shake the earth under her feet, she knew she had only one thing to do at that point. That was to, in her words, "run like hell" to the house as she would be chased by this poem. She had to get to a piece of paper fast enough so that when it thundered through her, she could collect it and grab it on the page. Other times she wouldn't be fast enough, so she would be running and running, and she wouldn't get to the house, and the poem would barrel through her and she would miss it, and it would "continue on across the landscape looking for another poet." Wikipedia article https://en.wikipedia.org/wiki/Ruth_Stone

Photo by: Julian Hochgesang on Unsplash

Photo by: Mark Cruz on Unsplash

RINGING OR HIGH PITCHED SOUNDS: If you hear a buzzing, ringing or high pitched sound and you can't for the life of you figure out where it is coming from, then this may be your Spirit Team talking to you. It may feel like one ear feels like it has cotton wool in it and then you hear this sound. Stop what you are doing in that moment, and take note of what you are thinking or saying. If it is disruptive or you dislike the sound, you can ask for your messages to be conveyed in a different way or you can simply say "yes, thank you, I have received your message", and the sound will stop. You will have received the audio download regardless of how long the sound goes on for.

Sometimes you may hear a sound and then get an inner knowing about what you were told. Sometimes you won't know straight away what was being conveyed. If you receive any other information along with the sounds, you may like to record it (either verbally or written) so you can refer back to it at a later date.

SONGS OR MUSIC PLAYING: If a song starts playing in your mind, or you turn the radio on and a song is playing, listen to the lyrics. Ask whether these lyrics are related to the question you have asked, the guidance you are seeking or a path you have been contemplating. There are clues in the words that you hear; if you can decode how they relate to your life, you will be guided on your way.

For example, a friend of mine had an old 80s TV theme song playing in her head for days, and she didn't know what it meant. Then we had a chat about what she wanted to do with an old business project she had shelved. That night, the song came flooding in and she realised it was giving her the answer she needed.

"Step by step, day by day, a fresh start over, a different hand to play. The deeper we fall, the stronger we stay, and we'll be better the second time around." - Step by Step, Sasha Mitchell

USING TELEPATHY TO COMMUNICATE: You might think you hear someone say something to you, so you turn towards them and then they ask you out loud what you just heard them say in your head. Or you might answer a question that you heard someone say, only to have them say in a surprised tone, *"I was just about to ask you about that!"*.

What to do when you are stuck

When you find yourself feeling overwhelmed, panicked, frustrated, angry, sad, hopeless, drowning...take a deep breath, and go somewhere where you can sit quietly.

The first thing you can do, is simply breathe; take a deep breath in for 5 counts, hold for 5 counts, and then breathe out for 5 counts, for 5 minutes.

When you are in this emotive space, it can be hard to access your intuition clearly. You need to get your body out of it's fight or flight response in order to hear what you need to hear to move forward.

Once you are feeling calmer, close your eyes and go within. You have access to your Spirit Team, who are ready and willing to assist you in any way you need, but you have to ask them. This is the key. They are causal beings and are not able to directly affect the physical realm. So in order get the inspiration, guidance, answers, feedback, etc that you require to make a decision, you must ask. When you ask for guidance, you need to look for the answers in a way that aligns with your Dominant Intuitive Language. If you want help with connecting to your Spirit Team, purchase our Meet Your Muse Meditation bundle https://lightcodelab.com/meetyourmuse). You may receive guidance in this space, or if you are out in the world, they may be physical/metaphysical signs.

Refer back to the previous pages where we explored these signs in more detail.

Alarms, horns, sirens, bells
Songs or music
Verbal instructions
Ringing, or high pitched sounds
Using telepathy to communicate

Seek these signs while asking questions of your Spirit Team. If you need to make a decision, ask "which option is for my highest good" or "give me a sign for what I need to do next to stay in flow and be on my path".

All choices will eventually lead you where you need to go, however, some may be quicker than others. Start to seek the signs that show you when you are in flow and when you are out of flow. If you can't understand the signs, join us in the Facebook group: MAGIC NOT LOGIC with Julie & Tash Lewin, where we assist with Decoding Signs & Signals. The more you practice, the easier and quicker you will interpret what is being shown.

How do you make the volume louder?

When you start out, it can be difficult to know whether you are just imagining what you are hearing or if it is really coming from the Universe. Knowing when you are connected in will be different for everyone, and so you will need to seek a confirmation that is unique to you.

If you hear a sound, song, noise, either in your mind or in the world, and you're not sure if it means anything, ask your Spirit Team to adjust the volume or make it clearer. If your instructions are too quiet or are staticky, simply ask for them to boost the signal and make it clearer for you.

You might ask your Spirit Team to communicate the same sign multiple times, if you want to be sure it is one. Or you may ask for the sign to be louder than everything else, or have a deeper resonance. If you only get fleeting sounds, which are too quick for you, ask your Spirit Team to slow them down, so you have more time to interpret them. If the symbolism (because that is how the Universe communicates) is too vague for you to understand, ask to be guided to resources that can help you interpret the symbols.

Like anything, accessing and using your Intuition in your business and daily life takes practice. You are learning a new language and like any new language, the integration into your vocabulary takes time. Be patient with yourself, and seek interpretation decoding in our free Facebook group **MAGIC NOT LOGIC with Julie & Tash Lewin**.

INTUITIVE LANGUAGE WORKSHEETS

Signs & Signals Tracking Sheets for

Clairaudience

CLEAR HEARING

SOUND EFFECTS IN THE WORLD

What sounds did you hear and take note of?

EXAMPLES:
Alarms, horns, sirens, bells, banging, bumps, drills, lawnmowers, animals calling, car brakes, vehicles...

What were you thinking about, contemplating or asking for guidance on when these occurred?

What revelations did you have when reflecting on the symbolism of these sounds?

SONGS OR MUSIC

What songs or music did you hear in the world or in your head that you took note of?

EXAMPLES:
Random song lyrics coming to mind, earworms, songs on the radio, song hooks or melodies...

What were you thinking about, contemplating or asking for guidance on when these occurred?

What revelations did you have when reflecting on the symbolism of these songs or music?

VERBAL INSTRUCTIONS

What did you hear and where did the voice come from? i.e. outside of you, inside your head

EXAMPLES:
Stop, slow down, be careful, turn around, you thought you couldn't do it, woohoo/cheering, full instructions of what to do...

What were you thinking about, contemplating or asking for guidance on before these occurred?

What revelations did you have when reflecting on the symbolism of these instructions?

RINGING OR HIGH PITCHED SOUND

What sounds did you hear or take note of?

EXAMPLES:
Muffled sound, cotton wool sound, angelic music, high pitched tone, staticky sound, crackly sound...

What were you thinking about, contemplating or asking for guidance on before/when these occurred?

What revelations did you have when reflecting on the meaning behind the sounds you heard?

TELEPATHIC MESSAGES

What thoughts or messages did you randomly hear and then have confirmed by those you were with?

EXAMPLES:
These are more verbal messages you hear from those around you; they may be random thoughts, requests, pondering...

What were you thinking about, contemplating or asking for guidance on before/when these occurred?

What revelations did you have when reflecting on what you heard?

SOUND EFFECTS IN THE WORLD

What sounds did you hear and take note of?

EXAMPLES:
Alarms, horns, sirens, bells, banging, bumps, drills, lawnmowers, animals calling, car brakes, vehicles...

What were you thinking about, contemplating or asking for guidance on when these occurred?

What revelations did you have when reflecting on the symbolism of these sounds?

SONGS OR MUSIC

What songs or music did you hear in the world or in your head that you took note of?

EXAMPLES:
Random song lyrics coming to mind, earworms, songs on the radio, song hooks or melodies...

What were you thinking about, contemplating or asking for guidance on when these occurred?

What revelations did you have when reflecting on the symbolism of these songs or music?

VERBAL INSTRUCTIONS

What did you hear and where did the voice come from? i.e. outside of you, inside your head

EXAMPLES:
Stop, slow down, be careful, turn around, you thought you couldn't do it, woohoo/cheering, full instructions of what to do...

What were you thinking about, contemplating or asking for guidance on before these occurred?

What revelations did you have when reflecting on the symbolism of these instructions?

RINGING OR HIGH PITCHED SOUND

What sounds did you hear or take note of?

EXAMPLES:
Muffled sound,
cotton wool sound,
angelic music,
high pitched tone,
staticky sound,
crackly sound...

What were you thinking about, contemplating or asking for guidance on before/when these occurred?

What revelations did you have when reflecting on the meaning behind the sounds you heard?

DAY 02

TELEPATHIC MESSAGES

What thoughts or messages did you randomly hear and then have confirmed by those you were with?

EXAMPLES:
These are more verbal messages you hear from those around you; they may be random thoughts, requests, pondering...

What were you thinking about, contemplating or asking for guidance on before/when these occurred?

What revelations did you have when reflecting on what you heard?

SOUND EFFECTS IN THE WORLD

What sounds did you hear and take note of?

EXAMPLES:
Alarms, horns, sirens, bells, banging, bumps, drills, lawnmowers, animals calling, car brakes, vehicles...

What were you thinking about, contemplating or asking for guidance on when these occurred?

What revelations did you have when reflecting on the symbolism of these sounds?

SONGS OR MUSIC

What songs or music did you hear in the world or in your head that you took note of?

EXAMPLES:
Random song lyrics coming to mind, earworms, songs on the radio, song hooks or melodies...

What were you thinking about, contemplating or asking for guidance on when these occurred?

What revelations did you have when reflecting on the symbolism of these songs or music?

VERBAL INSTRUCTIONS

What did you hear and where did the voice come from? i.e. outside of you, inside your head

EXAMPLES:
Stop, slow down, be careful, turn around, you thought you couldn't do it, woohoo/cheering, full instructions of what to do...

What were you thinking about, contemplating or asking for guidance on before these occurred?

What revelations did you have when reflecting on the symbolism of these instructions?

RINGING OR HIGH PITCHED SOUND

What sounds did you hear or take note of?

EXAMPLES:
Muffled sound,
cotton wool sound,
angelic music,
high pitched tone,
staticky sound,
crackly sound...

What were you thinking about, contemplating or asking for guidance on before/when these occurred?

What revelations did you have when reflecting on the meaning behind the sounds you heard?

TELEPATHIC MESSAGES

What thoughts or messages did you randomly hear and then have confirmed by those you were with?

EXAMPLES:
These are more verbal messages you hear from those around you; they may be random thoughts, requests, pondering...

What were you thinking about, contemplating or asking for guidance on before/when these occurred?

What revelations did you have when reflecting on what you heard?

SOUND EFFECTS IN THE WORLD

What sounds did you hear and take note of?

EXAMPLES:
Alarms, horns, sirens, bells, banging, bumps, drills, lawnmowers, animals calling, car brakes, vehicles...

What were you thinking about, contemplating or asking for guidance on when these occurred?

What revelations did you have when reflecting on the symbolism of these sounds?

SONGS OR MUSIC

What songs or music did you hear in the world or in your head that you took note of?

EXAMPLES:
Random song lyrics coming to mind, earworms, songs on the radio, song hooks or melodies...

What were you thinking about, contemplating or asking for guidance on when these occurred?

What revelations did you have when reflecting on the symbolism of these songs or music?

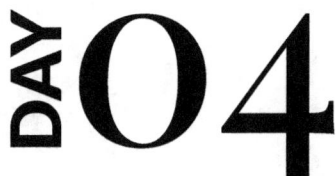

VERBAL INSTRUCTIONS

What did you hear and where did the voice come from? i.e. outside of you, inside your head

EXAMPLES:
Stop, slow down, be careful, turn around, you thought you couldn't do it, woohoo/cheering, full instructions of what to do...

What were you thinking about, contemplating or asking for guidance on before these occurred?

What revelations did you have when reflecting on the symbolism of these instructions?

RINGING OR HIGH PITCHED SOUND

What sounds did you hear or take note of?

EXAMPLES:
Muffled sound,
cotton wool sound,
angelic music,
high pitched tone,
staticky sound,
crackly sound...

What were you thinking about, contemplating or asking for guidance on before/when these occurred?

What revelations did you have when reflecting on the meaning behind the sounds you heard?

TELEPATHIC MESSAGES

What thoughts or messages did you randomly hear and then have confirmed by those you were with?

EXAMPLES:
These are more verbal messages you hear from those around you; they may be random thoughts, requests, pondering...

What were you thinking about, contemplating or asking for guidance on before/when these occurred?

What revelations did you have when reflecting on what you heard?

SOUND EFFECTS IN THE WORLD

What sounds did you hear and take note of?

EXAMPLES:
Alarms, horns, sirens, bells, banging, bumps, drills, lawnmowers, animals calling, car brakes, vehicles...

What were you thinking about, contemplating or asking for guidance on when these occurred?

What revelations did you have when reflecting on the symbolism of these sounds?

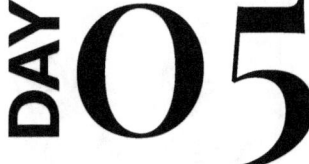

SONGS OR MUSIC

What songs or music did you hear in the world or in your head that you took note of?

EXAMPLES:
Random song lyrics coming to mind, earworms, songs on the radio, song hooks or melodies...

What were you thinking about, contemplating or asking for guidance on when these occurred?

What revelations did you have when reflecting on the symbolism of these songs or music?

VERBAL INSTRUCTIONS

What did you hear and where did the voice come from? i.e. outside of you, inside your head

EXAMPLES:
Stop, slow down, be careful, turn around, you thought you couldn't do it, woohoo/cheering, full instructions of what to do...

What were you thinking about, contemplating or asking for guidance on before these occurred?

What revelations did you have when reflecting on the symbolism of these instructions?

RINGING OR HIGH PITCHED SOUND

What sounds did you hear or take note of?

EXAMPLES:
Muffled sound, cotton wool sound, angelic music, high pitched tone, staticky sound, crackly sound...

What were you thinking about, contemplating or asking for guidance on before/when these occurred?

What revelations did you have when reflecting on the meaning behind the sounds you heard?

TELEPATHIC MESSAGES

What thoughts or messages did you randomly hear and then have confirmed by those you were with?

EXAMPLES:
These are more verbal messages you hear from those around you; they may be random thoughts, requests, pondering...

What were you thinking about, contemplating or asking for guidance on before/when these occurred?

What revelations did you have when reflecting on what you heard?

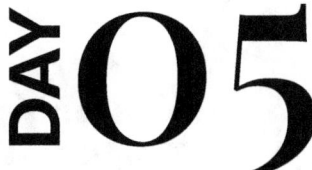

SOUND EFFECTS IN THE WORLD

What sounds did you hear and take note of?

EXAMPLES:
Alarms, horns, sirens, bells, banging, bumps, drills, lawnmowers, animals calling, car brakes, vehicles...

What were you thinking about, contemplating or asking for guidance on when these occurred?

What revelations did you have when reflecting on the symbolism of these sounds?

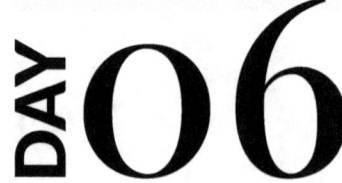

SONGS OR MUSIC

What songs or music did you hear in the world or in your head that you took note of?

EXAMPLES:
Random song lyrics coming to mind, earworms, songs on the radio, song hooks or melodies...

What were you thinking about, contemplating or asking for guidance on when these occurred?

What revelations did you have when reflecting on the symbolism of these songs or music?

VERBAL INSTRUCTIONS

What did you hear and where did the voice come from? i.e. outside of you, inside your head

EXAMPLES:
Stop, slow down, be careful, turn around, you thought you couldn't do it, woohoo/cheering, full instructions of what to do...

What were you thinking about, contemplating or asking for guidance on before these occurred?

What revelations did you have when reflecting on the symbolism of these instructions?

RINGING OR HIGH PITCHED SOUND

What sounds did you hear or take note of?

EXAMPLES:
Muffled sound,
cotton wool sound,
angelic music,
high pitched tone,
staticky sound,
crackly sound...

What were you thinking about, contemplating or asking for guidance on before/when these occurred?

What revelations did you have when reflecting on the meaning behind the sounds you heard?

TELEPATHIC MESSAGES

What thoughts or messages did you randomly hear and then have confirmed by those you were with?

EXAMPLES:
These are more verbal messages you hear from those around you; they may be random thoughts, requests, pondering...

What were you thinking about, contemplating or asking for guidance on before/when these occurred?

What revelations did you have when reflecting on what you heard?

SOUND EFFECTS IN THE WORLD

What sounds did you hear and take note of?

EXAMPLES:
Alarms, horns, sirens, bells, banging, bumps, drills, lawnmowers, animals calling, car brakes, vehicles...

What were you thinking about, contemplating or asking for guidance on when these occurred?

What revelations did you have when reflecting on the symbolism of these sounds?

SONGS OR MUSIC

What songs or music did you hear in the world or in your head that you took note of?

EXAMPLES:
Random song lyrics coming to mind, earworms, songs on the radio, song hooks or melodies...

What were you thinking about, contemplating or asking for guidance on when these occurred?

What revelations did you have when reflecting on the symbolism of these songs or music?

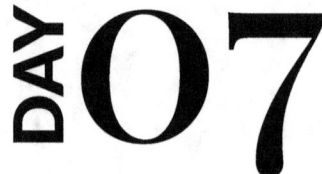

VERBAL INSTRUCTIONS

What did you hear and where did the voice come from? i.e. outside of you, inside your head

EXAMPLES:
Stop, slow down, be careful, turn around, you thought you couldn't do it, woohoo/cheering, full instructions of what to do...

What were you thinking about, contemplating or asking for guidance on before these occurred?

What revelations did you have when reflecting on the symbolism of these instructions?

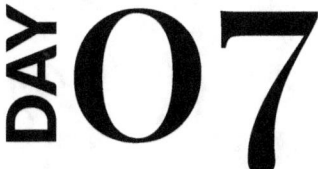

RINGING OR HIGH PITCHED SOUND

What sounds did you hear or take note of?

EXAMPLES:
Muffled sound, cotton wool sound, angelic music, high pitched tone, staticky sound, crackly sound...

What were you thinking about, contemplating or asking for guidance on before/when these occurred?

What revelations did you have when reflecting on the meaning behind the sounds you heard?

TELEPATHIC MESSAGES

What thoughts or messages did you randomly hear and then have confirmed by those you were with?

EXAMPLES:
These are more verbal messages you hear from those around you; they may be random thoughts, requests, pondering...

What were you thinking about, contemplating or asking for guidance on before/when these occurred?

What revelations did you have when reflecting on what you heard?

REFLECTION TIME

What did you discover about your Dominant Intuitive Language?

What signs & signals did you experience most often?

Did you access any of the other Dominant Intuitive Languages?

ACTIVITIES TO ENHANCE YOUR CONNECTION

When doing any tasks or activities where you are connecting with your Intuition, ask yourself: "What am I hearing physically and psychically?"

EXPLORING SOUND
1. Sit silently and focus your attention on yourself. You may do this activity out in nature, in your home, or wherever you feel comfortable
2. Focus your attention on the individual sounds that you can hear within 10m
3. Focus your attention on the individual sounds that you can hear within 50m, ignore the 10m sounds
4. Focus your attention on the individual sounds that you can hear within 200m, ignore the 10m & 50m sounds
5. Bring your attention back to you and see if you can still identify all of the individual sounds
6. Record any observations you made during the experience

KEEP A SYMBOLISM RECORD
1. Get a special notebook or journal just for this exercise or create a folder for voice memos
2. Record the sounds that you hear that make you take notice
3. Research the meaning and symbolism of these sounds to identify any patterns

LINKING OTHER SENSES TO SOUND
1. When you hear a sound, reflect on what other Senses you are accessing or experiencing
2. Record these observations in a journal or voice memos

HOW SOUND AFFECTS YOU
1. Take note of sounds that affect you physically
2. Journal or record how you are affected while the sound is playing and what happens to you after it stops. These may be positive and negative experiences

YOUR INTUITIVE LANGUAGE GUIDE

Your Dominant Intuitive Language is:
Clairsentience
CLEAR FEELING

"Everything I experience hits me deep, raw and intense. I feel the energy of myself and others. As I age, this ability only grows deeper & stranger."

– Sylvester McNutt III

Your Dominant Intuitive Language is:
Clairsentience
CLEAR FEELING

You are empathic. You feel it all; what is, has been and can be in the future. You deeply feel what you feel, what others feel and how the world feels. You work with the Subtle Realm, feeling into all that you come into contact with, allowing everyone to connect more deeply with their own feelings. You create peace and acceptance, it oozes out of you...a calming and sensual grace, that all who experience you, can't help but love. You draw them in, you create a safe place to fall apart and be made whole once more.

You have the extraordinary ability to receive intuitive impressions through feeling, in the form of emotions, physical touch & fleeting sensations. These may be physical in the world around you, within your body or within the energetic body. They may be detailed or a flash of impressions. You may receive these feelings while awake, in meditation, dreaming or in a lucid dream state.

The key differentiator for this Language type is that you FEEL things.

You use language like "Ah, yes, I feel you", "That feels great", "Urgh, I feel rough", "That feels so red, it's hot and burns", "Does that feeling belong to me?", "I feel your emotions", "It feels overwhelming, like I can't breathe", "I've got goosebumps", "That made me tear up", "You feel good"

To hone this ability and use it consciously during your co-creating work, continue reading.

93

Common Signs & Signals

EMOTIONS; YOURS AND OTHER PEOPLE'S: You will probably feel everything, at a very deep level. You may cry easily, empathise with other's pain, feel connected to everyone and everything, and sometimes have trouble separating what belongs to you, and what someone else is feeling. Knowing that the emotions you experience aren't always yours, can be very freeing.

So if you feel a strong emotion, that isn't sitting right, ask yourself *"does this emotion belong to me?"* If no, release it back to the person with love and light. If yes, ask yourself, *"does this emotion serve my highest good right now?"*. If no, release it from your physical and energetic bodies, back to the universe with gratitude, love and light. Emotions are an indicator and can be signposts for us to make different choices; however, you don't have to feel everything and hold onto it in order to get the lessons.

PHYSICAL SENSATIONS; GOOSEBUMPS, TINGLES, HEAT FLASHES, ENERGY, TEARS, CHOKED UP, TENSING MUSCLES: There may be different scenarios that trigger these physical sensations. You may get different signs when you are asking for your own confirmations vs other people. Differentiating these can be helpful to know whether they are your confirmations or not.

For example, when I am doing work with or for other people, and I start channelling information for them, I get strong rushes of energy, sometimes I choke up, I get goosebumps and tingles in various chakras. However, when I am getting my own confirmations I utilise my body pendulum when asking for assistance, and I will feel a rush of excitement when it is a yes, and a tensing of muscles when it is a no.

Photo by: Gabrielle Henderson on Unsplash

Photo by: Mark Adriane on Unsplash

FEELING PHYSICAL PAIN: If you feel pain in your body, this may be your own and you can intepret it. Or you may be tapping into another's pain or experience. Begin by asking your Spirit Team, "Is this pain a part of my own experience?" If the answer, is no, ask "does this belong to someone else?". If yes, "do I need to do anything with this feeling?"

If the pain is your own, you can then explore Metaphysical Body Language to determine what it is trying to tell you about a given situation.

For example, the pain in the shoulders can indicate that you have taken responsibility for a person or situation that isn't your own. You can acknowledge, and accept any lessons you are required to learn, and ask your Spirit Team to "release these emotions back to the Universe with love and light, so others may learn from them. They no longer serve me and no longer need to be stored in my energetic body. Thank you."

There are many examples of Metaphysical Body Language, download the free Guide from our website lightcodelab.com/metaphysical-body-language). More examples can also be found in Julie Lewin's book "The Art of Self-Healing. This can also be purchased on our shop.

RESPECTING THE VIBE YOU FEEL: You will feel the vibe of a person or place as a very real experience. Don't discount this vibe or allow others to minimise what you are feeling. You are connected into the subtle energy of the people and places you go, and you will feel if something is off. Trust this.

On the flip side, you will feel if you can trust someone you have just met. If it feels like you have known them forever, then you are connected into your timeless Akashic relationship.

Trust the vibes you feel.

What to do when you are stuck

When you find yourself feeling overwhelmed, panicked, frustrated, angry, sad, hopeless, drowning... take a deep breath, and go somewhere where you can sit quietly.

The first thing you can do, is simply breathe; take a deep breath in for 5 counts, hold for 5 counts, and then breathe out for 5 counts, for 5 minutes.

When you are in this emotive space, it can be hard to access your intuition clearly. You need to get your body out of it's fight or flight response in order to feel what you need to feel to move forward.

Once you are feeling calmer, close your eyes and go within. You have access to your Spirit Team, who are ready and willing to assist you in any way you need, but you have to ask them. This is the key. They are causal beings and are not able to directly affect the physical realm. So in order get the inspiration, guidance, answers, feedback, etc that you require to make a decision, you must ask. When you ask for guidance, you need to look for the answers in a way that aligns with your Dominant Intuitive Language. If you want help with connecting to your Spirit Team, purchase our Meet Your Muse Meditation bundle https://lightcodelab.com/meetyourmuse). You may receive guidance in this space, or if you are out in the world, they may be physical/metaphysical signs.

Refer back to the previous pages where we explored these signs in more detail.

Physical sensations
Emotions; yours and other people's
Vibe is very real to you
Feeling physical pain

Seek these signs while asking questions of your Spirit Team. If you need to make a decision, ask "which option is for my highest good" or "give me a sign for what I need to do next to stay in flow and be on my path".

All choices will eventually lead you where you need to go, however, some may be quicker than others. Start to seek the signs that show you when you are in flow and when you are out of flow. If you can't understand the signs, join us in the Facebook group: MAGIC NOT LOGIC with Julie & Tash Lewin, where we assist with Decoding Signs & Signals. The more you practice, the easier and quicker you will interpret what is being shown.

How do you make the feelings clearer?

When you start out, it can be difficult to know whether you are just imagining what you are feeling or if it is really coming from the Universe. Knowing when you are connected in will be different for everyone, and so you will need to seek a confirmation that is unique to you.

If you feel a physical or emotional sign, either in your body or from the world around you, and you're not sure if it means anything, ask your Spirit Team to make what you are feeling more obvious or stronger.

You might ask your Spirit Team to show you the same sign multiple times, if you want to be sure it is one. Or you may ask for the sign to be accompanied by other sensations; a physical sensation may be accompanied by an emotional reponse. If you only get flashes of emotions or sensations which are too quick for you, ask your Spirit Team to make the feelings last longer so you have more time to interpret them. If the symbolism (because that is how the Universe communicates) is too vague for you to understand, ask to be guided to resources that can help you interpret the symbols.

Like anything, accessing and using your Intuition in your business and daily life takes practice. You are learning a new language and like any new language, the integration into your vocabulary takes time. Be patient with yourself, and seek interpretation decoding in our free Facebook group MAGIC NOT LOGIC with Julie & Tash Lewin.

INTUITIVE LANGUAGE WORKSHEETS

Signs & Signals Tracking Sheets for

Clairsentience

CLEAR FEELING

PHYSICAL SENSATIONS

What physical sensations did you feel and take note of?

EXAMPLES:
Goosebumps, tingles, heat flashes, energy, tears, choked up, tensing muscles...

What were you thinking about, contemplating or asking for guidance on when these occurred?

What revelations did you have when reflecting on the symbolism of these sensations?

EMOTIONS: YOURS + OTHER'S

What emotions did you feel in your body, whether physically or emotionally?

EXAMPLES:
You might feel physical sensations you associate with that emotion e.g. hot when angry, cold when fearful, tingling when loving, tearful when sad...

What were you thinking about, contemplating or asking for guidance on when these occurred?

What revelations did you have when reflecting on the symbolism of these emotions?

THE GENERAL VIBE

What were you doing or who were you with when you felt a vibe that was either good or was off?

EXAMPLES:
You may tap into the general vibe of people, places or things. It might be hard to describe this, so think of some metaphors or symbols.

What were you thinking about, contemplating or asking for guidance on before/when these occurred?

What revelations did you have when reflecting on the symbolism of these feelings?

FEELING PHYSICAL PAIN

What areas of your body did you experience pain? Was it your pain or were you tapping into someone else?

EXAMPLES:
You might feel pain in your body that is yours or someone else's. Explore the Metaphysical Body Language (free Guide on our website lightcodelab.com/metaphysical-body-language) for these areas of your body.

What were you thinking about, contemplating or asking for guidance on before/when these occurred?

What revelations did you have when reflecting on the meaning behind the pain you were feeling and where it was located?

PHYSICAL SENSATIONS

What physical sensations did you feel and take note of?

EXAMPLES:
Goosebumps, tingles, heat flashes, energy, tears, choked up, tensing muscles...

What were you thinking about, contemplating or asking for guidance on when these occurred?

What revelations did you have when reflecting on the symbolism of these sensations?

EMOTIONS: YOURS + OTHER'S

What emotions did you feel in your body, whether physically or emotionally?

EXAMPLES:
You might feel physical sensations you associate with that emotion e.g. hot when angry, cold when fearful, tingling when loving, tearful when sad...

What were you thinking about, contemplating or asking for guidance on when these occurred?

What revelations did you have when reflecting on the symbolism of these emotions?

THE GENERAL VIBE

What were you doing or who were you with when you felt a vibe that was either good or was off?

EXAMPLES:
You may tap into the general vibe of people, places or things. It might be hard to describe this, so think of some metaphors or symbols.

What were you thinking about, contemplating or asking for guidance on before/when these occurred?

What revelations did you have when reflecting on the symbolism of these feelings?

FEELING PHYSICAL PAIN

What areas of your body did you experience pain? Was it your pain or were you tapping into someone else?

EXAMPLES:
You might feel pain in your body that is yours or someone else's. Explore the Metaphysical Body Language (free Guide on our website lightcodelab.com/metaphysical-body-language) for these areas of your body.

What were you thinking about, contemplating or asking for guidance on before/when these occurred?

What revelations did you have when reflecting on the meaning behind the pain you were feeling and where it was located?

PHYSICAL SENSATIONS

What physical sensations did you feel and take note of?

EXAMPLES:
Goosebumps, tingles, heat flashes, energy, tears, choked up, tensing muscles...

What were you thinking about, contemplating or asking for guidance on when these occurred?

What revelations did you have when reflecting on the symbolism of these sensations?

EMOTIONS: YOURS + OTHER'S

What emotions did you feel in your body, whether physically or emotionally?

EXAMPLES:
You might feel physical sensations you associate with that emotion e.g. hot when angry, cold when fearful, tingling when loving, tearful when sad...

What were you thinking about, contemplating or asking for guidance on when these occurred?

What revelations did you have when reflecting on the symbolism of these emotions?

THE GENERAL VIBE

What were you doing or who were you with when you felt a vibe that was either good or was off?

EXAMPLES:
You may tap into the general vibe of people, places or things. It might be hard to describe this, so think of some metaphors or symbols.

What were you thinking about, contemplating or asking for guidance on before/when these occurred?

What revelations did you have when reflecting on the symbolism of these feelings?

FEELING PHYSICAL PAIN

What areas of your body did you experience pain? Was it your pain or were you tapping into someone else?

EXAMPLES:
You might feel pain in your body that is yours or someone else's. Explore the Metaphysical Body Language (free Guide on our website lightcodelab.com/metaphysical-body-language) for these areas of your body.

What were you thinking about, contemplating or asking for guidance on before/when these occurred?

What revelations did you have when reflecting on the meaning behind the pain you were feeling and where it was located?

PHYSICAL SENSATIONS

What physical sensations did you feel and take note of?

EXAMPLES:
Goosebumps, tingles, heat flashes, energy, tears, choked up, tensing muscles...

What were you thinking about, contemplating or asking for guidance on when these occurred?

What revelations did you have when reflecting on the symbolism of these sensations?

EMOTIONS: YOURS + OTHER'S

What emotions did you feel in your body, whether physically or emotionally?

EXAMPLES:
You might feel physical sensations you associate with that emotion e.g. hot when angry, cold when fearful, tingling when loving, tearful when sad...

What were you thinking about, contemplating or asking for guidance on when these occurred?

What revelations did you have when reflecting on the symbolism of these emotions?

THE GENERAL VIBE

What were you doing or who were you with when you felt a vibe that was either good or was off?

EXAMPLES:
You may tap into the general vibe of people, places or things. It might be hard to describe this, so think of some metaphors or symbols.

What were you thinking about, contemplating or asking for guidance on before/when these occurred?

What revelations did you have when reflecting on the symbolism of these feelings?

FEELING PHYSICAL PAIN

What areas of your body did you experience pain? Was it your pain or were you tapping into someone else?

EXAMPLES:
You might feel pain in your body that is yours or someone else's. Explore the Metaphysical Body Language (free Guide on our website [lightcodelab.com/metaphysical-body-language)](lightcodelab.com/metaphysical-body-language) for these areas of your body.

What were you thinking about, contemplating or asking for guidance on before/when these occurred?

What revelations did you have when reflecting on the meaning behind the pain you were feeling and where it was located?

PHYSICAL SENSATIONS

What physical sensations did you feel and take note of?

EXAMPLES:
Goosebumps, tingles, heat flashes, energy, tears, choked up, tensing muscles...

What were you thinking about, contemplating or asking for guidance on when these occurred?

What revelations did you have when reflecting on the symbolism of these sensations?

EMOTIONS: YOURS + OTHER'S

What emotions did you feel in your body, whether physically or emotionally?

EXAMPLES:
You might feel physical sensations you associate with that emotion e.g. hot when angry, cold when fearful, tingling when loving, tearful when sad...

What were you thinking about, contemplating or asking for guidance on when these occurred?

What revelations did you have when reflecting on the symbolism of these emotions?

THE GENERAL VIBE

What were you doing or who were you with when you felt a vibe that was either good or was off?

EXAMPLES:
You may tap into the general vibe of people, places or things. It might be hard to describe this, so think of some metaphors or symbols.

What were you thinking about, contemplating or asking for guidance on before/when these occurred?

What revelations did you have when reflecting on the symbolism of these feelings?

FEELING PHYSICAL PAIN

What areas of your body did you experience pain? Was it your pain or were you tapping into someone else?

EXAMPLES:
You might feel pain in your body that is yours or someone else's. Explore the Metaphysical Body Language (free Guide on our website lightcodelab.com/metaphysical-body-language) for these areas of your body.

What were you thinking about, contemplating or asking for guidance on before/when these occurred?

What revelations did you have when reflecting on the meaning behind the pain you were feeling and where it was located?

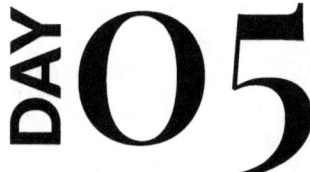

PHYSICAL SENSATIONS

What physical sensations did you feel and take note of?

EXAMPLES:
Goosebumps, tingles, heat flashes, energy, tears, choked up, tensing muscles...

What were you thinking about, contemplating or asking for guidance on when these occurred?

What revelations did you have when reflecting on the symbolism of these sensations?

EMOTIONS: YOURS + OTHER'S

What emotions did you feel in your body, whether physically or emotionally?

EXAMPLES:
You might feel physical sensations you associate with that emotion e.g. hot when angry, cold when fearful, tingling when loving, tearful when sad...

What were you thinking about, contemplating or asking for guidance on when these occurred?

What revelations did you have when reflecting on the symbolism of these emotions?

THE GENERAL VIBE

What were you doing or who were you with when you felt a vibe that was either good or was off?

EXAMPLES:
You may tap into the general vibe of people, places or things. It might be hard to describe this, so think of some metaphors or symbols.

What were you thinking about, contemplating or asking for guidance on before/when these occurred?

What revelations did you have when reflecting on the symbolism of these feelings?

FEELING PHYSICAL PAIN

What areas of your body did you experience pain? Was it your pain or were you tapping into someone else?

EXAMPLES:
You might feel pain in your body that is yours or someone else's. Explore the Metaphysical Body Language (free Guide on our website lightcodelab.com/metaphysical-body-language) for these areas of your body.

What were you thinking about, contemplating or asking for guidance on before/when these occurred?

What revelations did you have when reflecting on the meaning behind the pain you were feeling and where it was located?

PHYSICAL SENSATIONS

What physical sensations did you feel and take note of?

EXAMPLES:
Goosebumps, tingles, heat flashes, energy, tears, choked up, tensing muscles...

What were you thinking about, contemplating or asking for guidance on when these occurred?

What revelations did you have when reflecting on the symbolism of these sensations?

EMOTIONS: YOURS + OTHER'S

What emotions did you feel in your body, whether physically or emotionally?

EXAMPLES:
You might feel physical sensations you associate with that emotion e.g. hot when angry, cold when fearful, tingling when loving, tearful when sad...

What were you thinking about, contemplating or asking for guidance on when these occurred?

What revelations did you have when reflecting on the symbolism of these emotions?

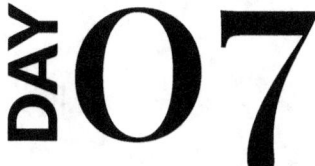

THE GENERAL VIBE

What were you doing or who were you with when you felt a vibe that was either good or was off?

EXAMPLES:
You may tap into the general vibe of people, places or things. It might be hard to describe this, so think of some metaphors or symbols.

What were you thinking about, contemplating or asking for guidance on before/when these occurred?

What revelations did you have when reflecting on the symbolism of these feelings?

FEELING PHYSICAL PAIN

What areas of your body did you experience pain? Was it your pain or were you tapping into someone else?

EXAMPLES:
You might feel pain in your body that is yours or someone else's. Explore the Metaphysical Body Language (free Guide on our website lightcodelab.com/metaphysical-body-language) for these areas of your body.

What were you thinking about, contemplating or asking for guidance on before/when these occurred?

What revelations did you have when reflecting on the meaning behind the pain you were feeling and where it was located?

REFLECTION TIME

What did you discover about your Dominant Intuitive Language?

What signs & signals did you experience most often?

Did you access any of the other Dominant Intuitive Languages?

ACTIVITIES TO ENHANCE YOUR CONNECTION

When doing any tasks or activities where you are connecting with your Intuition, ask yourself: "What am I feeling physically, emotionally and psychically?"

TACTILE EXPERIENCE
1. Collect a range of textures; food, nature, materials
2. Close your eyes and identify what these feel like physically, emotionally and any memories these trigger
    Physical: rough, smooth, hot, cold, wet, dry, heavy, light...
    Emotions: disgust, sensuality, care, comfort, happy, sad...
3. This will enhance your feeling signals, so record anything you are feeling and what it triggers in you

KNOWING WHAT BELONGS TO YOU
1. Sit quietly and close your eyes
2. Take 3 deep breaths
3. Ask your Spirit Team:
    "Does this emotion or feeling belong to me?"
If no, say:
    "I release you back to the owner with love and light"
If yes, ask:
    "Does this emotion serve my highest good?"
If no, say:
    "I release this emotion from all my subtle bodies back to the universe so lessons may be learnt there"

MAKING CHOICES
When faced with a dilemma or choice to make, do the following:
1. Identify what a yes feels like, and what a no feels like
2. Ask your body for a "YES" and a "NO" confirmation, identify what this feels like in your body; *This may be, emotions, sensations, movement*
3. Tune into a choice you have to make, ask your body
    "is saying yes to this in my highest good?"
4. Which physical confirmation do you get?

YOUR INTUITIVE LANGUAGE GUIDE

Your Dominant Intuitive Language is:
Clairalience
CLEAR SMELLING

"Nothing brings to life again a forgotton memory, like fragrance."

– Christopher Poindexter

Your Dominant Intuitive Language is:
Clairalience
CLEAR SMELLING

You are an evocateur. You are deeply connected to the world, memory, past, present and future through your sense of smell. You can trigger memories through physical scents, and you can be connected to people and events by calling on psychically perceived scents. You can call on intuitive knowledge through fragrance. You use scent as a confirmation signal, when connecting to those who have passed or your Spirit Team.

You have the extraordinary ability to receive intuitive impressions through smell, in the form of wafts of scent or memory triggers. These may be physical in the world around you or perceived psychically. They may be detailed or a flash of impressions. You may receive these scents while awake, in meditation, dreaming or in a lucid dream state.

The key differentiator for this Language type is that you SMELL things.

You use language like "Can you smell that", "Oh, grandma is here, I smell roses", "Is someone smoking?", "Is something burning?", "What's that smell?", "Where's that smell coming from?"

To hone this ability and use it consciously during your co-creating work, continue reading.

130

131

Common Signs & Signals

WAFTS OF SCENT WITH NO PHYSICAL SOURCE: Some common scents are, roses, lavender, violets, cigarette, cigar or marijuana smoke, perfume.

For example, my grandmother, who had passed, used to wear violet perfume, so whenever mum used to smell violets, we knew Grandma Rose was around. I regularly smell both cigarettes and marijuana (when no one is around), and know that my Grandpa (who use to smoke cigarettes) and my Great Grandpa (who used to smoke Pot) are around. I would be driving alone at night, and for a few kilometers, the car would be filled with the smell of Pot, and then suddenly it would be gone. I always thanked Grandpa for looking out for me and keeping me safe.

SMELLING WHAT YOU SEE: Sometimes the scents that I get, have nothing to do with being a sign, it is simply that I am so connected to my Clairalience in that moment, that I smell whatever I see.

For example, looking at this image of cigarettes, I can immediately smell that stale cigarette butt scent. I am taken back to riding in the car with my best friend as she drove us down the coast. I experience the same emotional intensity I felt on the day I stepped into her car and the stale cigarette smell wafted out the passenger door. I sat down and she lit up a fresh one, I felt connected to her and my life in a visceral way. All of that wafts over me as I look at this image and smell what I smelt on that day.

Photo by: Sara Kurfess on Unsplash

Photo by: Samantha Gades on Unsplash

If you receive visions when you smell certain scents, you are accessing your Clairvoyance. These may be visual memories associated with the scent triggers, or you may be accessing psychic perceptions and visions, provided to you through your Clairalience.

If these other senses are only triggered by smell or scents, then you can be sure your Dominant Intuitive Language is Clairalience. If you find you are accessing Clairalience as a result of one of the othe senses, then it may be a Secondary Language. Remember, we do have access to all of the senses, however, messages will be more clearly accessed if you practice your dominant sense.

LINKED TO OTHER SENSES:

This Clair sense is often linked with experiences of the other senses.

For example, if you are accessing intuitive knowledge (Claircognizance), you may get an information download when you smell a certain scent.

When you feel emotions based on a specific scent, you are accessing your clear feeling (Clairsentience). This can be useful if you are receiving psychic scents, to know what else is being perceived and gathering further information. Memories are most often built on emotions, and scent can trigger memories, therefore you will often be accessing both Clairalience and Clairsentience at these times.

What to do when you are stuck

When you find yourself feeling overwhelmed, panicked, frustrated, angry, sad, hopeless, drowning... take a deep breath, and go somewhere where you can sit quietly.

The first thing you can do, is simply breathe; take a deep breath in for 5 counts, hold for 5 counts, and then breathe out for 5 counts, for 5 minutes.

When you are in this emotive space, it can be hard to access your intuition clearly. You need to get your body out of it's fight or flight response in order to smell what you need to smell to move forward.

Once you are feeling calmer, close your eyes and go within. You have access to your Spirit Team, who are ready and willing to assist you in any way you need, but you have to ask them. This is the key. They are causal beings and are not able to directly affect the physical realm. So in order get the inspiration, guidance, answers, feedback, etc that you require to make a decision, you must ask. When you ask for guidance, you need to look for the answers in a way that aligns with your Dominant Intuitive Language. If you want help with connecting to your Spirit Team, purchase our Meet Your Muse Meditation bundle https://lightcodelab.com/meetyourmuse). You may receive guidance in this space, or if you are out in the world, they may be physical/metaphysical signs.

Refer back to the previous pages where we explored these signs in more detail.

Wafts of scent
Smelling what you see
Linked to the other Senses

Seek these signs while asking questions of your Spirit Team. If you need to make a decision, ask "which option is for my highest good" or "give me a sign for what I need to do next to stay in flow and be on my path".

All choices will eventually lead you where you need to go, however, some may be quicker than others. Start to seek the signs that show you when you are in flow and when you are out of flow. If you can't understand the signs, join us in the Facebook group: **MAGIC NOT LOGIC with Julie & Tash Lewin**, where we assist with Decoding Signs & Signals. The more you practice, the easier and quicker you will interpret what is being shown.

How do you make the scent clearer?

When you start out, it can be difficult to know whether you are just imagining what you are smelling or if it is really coming from the Universe. Knowing when you are connected in will be different for everyone, and so you will need to seek a confirmation that is unique to you.

For intuitive guidance, you will likely be getting non-physical scents. If these scents waft over you, with no associated information or you're just not sure what they mean, ask your Spirit Team to provide you with additional connections, memories or information. As a sign of confirmation, you may connect with physical scents, ones that are actually in the world around you. If they are particularly strong, or they bring up emotions or memories, then it is important to take note of them.

If you need the scents to be clearer, or more pungent for you to use them as triggers, then ask your Spirit Team to make them more obvious in whatever way you need. If you want to incorporate another associated Language, then ask them to assist you in developing whichever Secondary Language comes most naturally to you.

Like anything, accessing and using your Intuition in your business and daily life takes practice. You are learning a new language and like any new language, the integration into your vocabulary takes time. Be patient with yourself, and seek interpretation decoding in our free Facebook group MAGIC NOT LOGIC with Julie & Tash Lewin.

INTUITIVE LANGUAGE WORKSHEETS

Signs & Signals Tracking Sheets for

Clairalience

CLEAR SMELLING

WAFTS OF SCENT OR FRAGRANCE

What did you smell, either physically or psychically and take note of?

EXAMPLES:
Roses, lavender, violets, cigarette, cigar or marijuana smoke, perfume...

What were you thinking about, contemplating or asking for guidance on when these occurred?

What revelations did you have when reflecting on the symbolism of these smells?

SMELLING WHAT YOU SEE

What were you looking at that caused you to psychically smell it and take note of?

EXAMPLES:
Any experience where you see something physically and then psychically smell it.

What were you thinking about, contemplating or asking for guidance on when these occurred?

What revelations did you have when reflecting on the symbolism of what you saw and smelled?

LINKED TO OTHER SENSES

What other experiences did you have, after originally smelling something either physically or psychically?

EXAMPLES:
When you either see, hear, feel or know something straight after you have Smelled something physically or psychically.

What were you thinking about, contemplating or asking for guidance on before/when these occurred?

What revelations did you have when reflecting on the symbolism of multi-sense experiences?

WAFTS OF SCENT OR FRAGRANCE

What did you smell, either physically or psychically and take note of?

EXAMPLES:
Roses, lavender, violets, cigarette, cigar or marijuana smoke, perfume...

What were you thinking about, contemplating or asking for guidance on when these occurred?

What revelations did you have when reflecting on the symbolism of these smells?

SMELLING WHAT YOU SEE

What were you looking at that caused you to psychically smell it and take note of?

EXAMPLES:
Any experience where you see something physically and then psychically smell it.

What were you thinking about, contemplating or asking for guidance on when these occurred?

What revelations did you have when reflecting on the symbolism of what you saw and smelled?

LINKED TO OTHER SENSES

What other experiences did you have, after originally smelling something either physically or psychically?

EXAMPLES:
When you either see, hear, feel or know something straight after you have Smelled something physically or psychically.

What were you thinking about, contemplating or asking for guidance on before/when these occurred?

What revelations did you have when reflecting on the symbolism of multi-sense experiences?

WAFTS OF SCENT OR FRAGRANCE

What did you smell, either physically or psychically and take note of?

EXAMPLES:
Roses, lavender, violets, cigarette, cigar or marijuana smoke, perfume...

What were you thinking about, contemplating or asking for guidance on when these occurred?

What revelations did you have when reflecting on the symbolism of these smells?

SMELLING WHAT YOU SEE

What were you looking at that caused you to psychically smell it and take note of?

EXAMPLES:
Any experience where you see something physically and then psychically smell it.

What were you thinking about, contemplating or asking for guidance on when these occurred?

What revelations did you have when reflecting on the symbolism of what you saw and smelled?

LINKED TO OTHER SENSES

What other experiences did you have, after originally smelling something either physically or psychically?

EXAMPLES:
When you either see, hear, feel or know something straight after you have Smelled something physically or psychically.

What were you thinking about, contemplating or asking for guidance on before/when these occurred?

What revelations did you have when reflecting on the symbolism of multi-sense experiences?

WAFTS OF SCENT OR FRAGRANCE

What did you smell, either physically or psychically and take note of?

EXAMPLES:
Roses, lavender, violets, cigarette, cigar or marijuana smoke, perfume...

What were you thinking about, contemplating or asking for guidance on when these occurred?

What revelations did you have when reflecting on the symbolism of these smells?

SMELLING WHAT YOU SEE

What were you looking at that caused you to psychically smell it and take note of?

EXAMPLES:
Any experience where you see something physically and then psychically smell it.

What were you thinking about, contemplating or asking for guidance on when these occurred?

What revelations did you have when reflecting on the symbolism of what you saw and smelled?

LINKED TO OTHER SENSES

What other experiences did you have, after originally smelling something either physically or psychically?

EXAMPLES:
When you either see, hear, feel or know something straight after you have Smelled something physically or psychically.

What were you thinking about, contemplating or asking for guidance on before/when these occurred?

What revelations did you have when reflecting on the symbolism of multi-sense experiences?

WAFTS OF SCENT OR FRAGRANCE

What did you smell, either physically or psychically and take note of?

EXAMPLES:
Roses, lavender, violets, cigarette, cigar or marijuana smoke, perfume...

What were you thinking about, contemplating or asking for guidance on when these occurred?

What revelations did you have when reflecting on the symbolism of these smells?

SMELLING WHAT YOU SEE

What were you looking at that caused you to psychically smell it and take note of?

EXAMPLES:
Any experience where you see something physically and then psychically smell it.

What were you thinking about, contemplating or asking for guidance on when these occurred?

What revelations did you have when reflecting on the symbolism of what you saw and smelled?

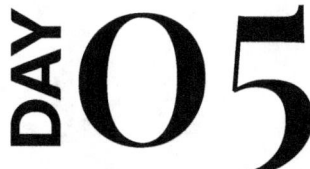

LINKED TO OTHER SENSES

What other experiences did you have, after originally smelling something either physically or psychically?

EXAMPLES:
When you either see, hear, feel or know something straight after you have Smelled something physically or psychically.

What were you thinking about, contemplating or asking for guidance on before/when these occurred?

What revelations did you have when reflecting on the symbolism of multi-sense experiences?

WAFTS OF SCENT OR FRAGRANCE

What did you smell, either physically or psychically and take note of?

EXAMPLES:
Roses, lavender, violets, cigarette, cigar or marijuana smoke, perfume...

What were you thinking about, contemplating or asking for guidance on when these occurred?

What revelations did you have when reflecting on the symbolism of these smells?

SMELLING WHAT YOU SEE

What were you looking at that caused you to psychically smell it and take note of?

EXAMPLES:
Any experience where you see something physically and then psychically smell it.

What were you thinking about, contemplating or asking for guidance on when these occurred?

What revelations did you have when reflecting on the symbolism of what you saw and smelled?

LINKED TO OTHER SENSES

What other experiences did you have, after originally smelling something either physically or psychically?

EXAMPLES:
When you either see, hear, feel or know something straight after you have Smelled something physically or psychically.

What were you thinking about, contemplating or asking for guidance on before/when these occurred?

What revelations did you have when reflecting on the symbolism of multi-sense experiences?

WAFTS OF SCENT OR FRAGRANCE

What did you smell, either physically or psychically and take note of?

EXAMPLES:
Roses, lavender, violets, cigarette, cigar or marijuana smoke, perfume...

What were you thinking about, contemplating or asking for guidance on when these occurred?

What revelations did you have when reflecting on the symbolism of these smells?

SMELLING WHAT YOU SEE

What were you looking at that caused you to psychically smell it and take note of?

EXAMPLES:
Any experience where you see something physically and then psychically smell it.

What were you thinking about, contemplating or asking for guidance on when these occurred?

What revelations did you have when reflecting on the symbolism of what you saw and smelled?

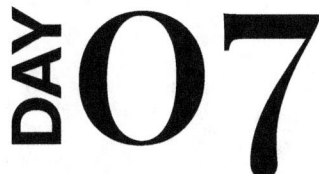

LINKED TO OTHER SENSES

What other experiences did you have, after originally smelling something either physically or psychically?

EXAMPLES:
When you either see, hear, feel or know something straight after you have Smelled something physically or psychically.

What were you thinking about, contemplating or asking for guidance on before/when these occurred?

What revelations did you have when reflecting on the symbolism of multi-sense experiences?

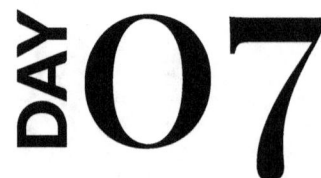

REFLECTION TIME

What did you discover about your Dominant Intuitive Language?

What signs & signals did you experience most often?

Did you access any of the other Dominant Intuitive Languages?

ACTIVITIES TO ENHANCE YOUR CONNECTION

When doing any tasks or activities where you are connecting with your Intuition, ask yourself: "What am I smelling physically and psychically?"

USE ESSENTIAL OILS
1. Take an essential oil and sniff from the bottle
2. Reflect on any emotions that rise up
3. Reflect on any memories that occur; *identify how you experience these i.e. visual, feelings, physical sensations, sounds, knowledge*
4. Record these in your preferred way

WRITE A MEMORY JOURNAL
1. Get a special notebook or journal just for this exercise
2. Reflect on memories that spring to mind based on the following word prompts:
    Mowing the lawn, best friend, primary school, first love, first heartbreak, first time seeing snow, first time travelling...add your own prompts as they come to you
3. Write down any smells that come to you when you reflect on those words and memories. You can write the accompanying memory if you wish, though this isn't essential

IMAGE-SCENT ASSOCIATION
1. Collect some images, either physical or digital
2. Get your journal or digital recording device of choice
3. Reflect on each image and identify any psychic smells you experience
4. Record what the image was and what/if you smelled it

YOUR INTUITIVE LANGUAGE GUIDE

Your Dominant Intuitive Language is:
Claircognizance
CLEAR KNOWING

> "When you don't know how you know... But you know you know... and you know you knew and that's all you needed to know..."

– Zen to Zany, The Mind's Journal

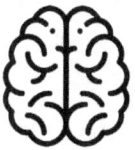

Your Dominant Intuitive Language is:
Claircognizance
CLEAR KNOWING

You are an enlightener. You have a direct line to the Akashic and Universal Flow. You seek to know, and you just do. You tap into past, present, and future possibilities, bringing to the world the information it needs to make them manifest. You may not know what this looks like but you know it exists, somewhere and somewhen. You know that you will meet the person who is meant to create what you know, which may in fact be you, in it's right time.

You have the extraordinary ability to receive downloads of information. You just know, and you can rarely explain how you know. You receive information for yourself, sometimes for others. You may get detailed information downloads, or fleeting thoughts pass through. You may receive these downloads while awake, in meditation, dreaming or in a lucid dream state.

The key differentiator for this Language type is that you just KNOW things.

You use language like "Yeah, I know", "I don't know how, but I just know", "I had a download", "I told you so", "I know what you mean", "I understand", "I get it".

To hone this ability and use it consciously during your co-creating work, continue reading.

162

Common Signs & Signals

IDEAS POP INTO YOUR HEAD OUT OF NOWHERE: This is probably the most common signal. You might be working on a project, creating something, or talking to people. And before you've thought it through an idea has lightbulbed into your mind and you have blurted it out. Normal thoughts and ideas will meander and flow, while a claircognizant idea will be like a lightening bolt, it will drop in hot off the press. It will sizzle with potential and you know it came from outside of you.

SPONTANEOUS ACTIONS: Without thought, you do something, and then upon reflection you realise what exactly that meant. This will often be part of a protective instinct.

For example, you are driving along, when suddenly you take the next exit, even though it will add time to your journey. When you reach your destination, you turn on the news and discover that there was an accident right where and when you were in the spot. Had you not exited when you did, you would have been caught up in the accident.

YOU KNOW WHERE YOU ARE EVEN WHEN YOU HAVEN'T BEEN THERE: Your sense of direction is on point, and you always know how to return to somewhere you've been. But, on occasion you even know where you are, even when you have never been there. It's like you have downloaded a map of the area, and you know how to get around.

Photo by: Timothy Perry on Unsplash

by: Jamie Streeton on Unsplash

PICKING UP PHONE BEFORE IT RINGS OR PINGS A MESSAGE: Have you ever picked up your phone, sure that it has made a sound only to find nothing there? But seconds later, it rings or pings.

For example, I do this one the most frequently of any. I will always pick up my phone, expecting a message, only to find there isn't one. Then a second later, the message comes in. It's like I connect into the intention, which has a delay through the technological channel, but I have already received it.

Be aware of whether you are "hearing" the message, or just knowing, they can be similar.

THINKING OF SOMEONE AND THEN THEY MAKE CONTACT: Have you ever had someone pop into your mind, and then they'll either get in contact or you will see them while you are out and about. This can happen with things as well as people. You could get an idea or thought pop into your mind, and then before you know it, that thing shows up in your world. You are a master manifester.

INFORMATION DOWNLOAD: This can be in the form of a flash of inspiration or information that you need in response to the world around you.

Or you could use this when doing Automatic Writing. This involves connecting to the Universe and becoming an open Channel, allowing information to pass directly through you to the page.

For example, I will often decide I want to learn a new skill. So I will casually watch a few videos, then when I make my first attempt, it's like I have plugged directly into the Matrix and I know how to do it. And not just do it poorly, do it well enough that I wonder if I had actually learnt how in the past/a past life.

What to do when you are stuck

When you find yourself feeling overwhelmed, panicked, frustrated, angry, sad, hopeless, drowning... take a deep breath, and go somewhere where you can sit quietly.

The first thing you can do, is simply breathe; take a deep breath in for 5 counts, hold for 5 counts, and then breathe out for 5 counts, for 5 minutes.

When you are in this emotive space, it can be hard to access your intuition clearly. You need to get your body out of it's fight or flight response in order to know what you need to know to move forward.

Once you are feeling calmer, close your eyes and go within. You have access to your Spirit Team, who are ready and willing to assist you in any way you need, but you have to ask them. This is the key. They are causal beings and are not able to directly affect the physical realm. So in order get the inspiration, guidance, answers, feedback, etc that you require to make a decision, you must ask. When you ask for guidance, you need to look for the answers in a way that aligns with your Dominant Intuitive Language. If you want help with connecting to your Spirit Team, purchase our Meet Your Muse Meditation bundle https://lightcodelab.com/meetyourmuse). You may receive guidance in this space, or if you are out in the world, they may be physical/metaphysical signs.

Refer back to the previous pages where we explored these signs in more detail.

Ideas pop into your head
Spontanous actions
Information downloads
Knowing before receiving msg's
Knowing where you are in unfamiliar places

Seek these signs while asking questions of your Spirit Team. If you need to make a decision, ask "which option is for my highest good" or "give me a sign for what I need to do next to stay in flow and be on my path".

All choices will eventually lead you where you need to go, however, some may be quicker than others. Start to seek the signs that show you when you are in flow and when you are out of flow. If you can't understand the signs, join us in the Facebook group: **MAGIC NOT LOGIC with Julie & Tash Lewin**, where we assist with Decoding Signs & Signals. The more you practice, the easier and quicker you will interpret what is being shown.

How do you receive clearer downloads?

When you start out, it can be difficult to know whether you are just imagining what you are knowing or if it is really coming from the Universe. Knowing when you are connected in will be different for everyone, and so you will need to seek a confirmation that is unique to you.

If you find that you just know something and you can't explain how you know it, or you get downloads of information just pop into your mind, it can be challenging to know whether this is just your imagination or if you are really being given this knowledge from outside of yourself. If you need assistance in trusting what you know or if it isn't in a useful format, ask for the information to be clearer or more specific.

You might ask them to provide the same information more than once. Or you may ask for the sign to be accompanied by other information or ideas. If you only get flashes of information, that disappear quickly, ask them to slow down the downloads so you have more time to interpret them. Or ask them to provide additional information that aids your interpretation. If the symbolism (because that is how the Universe communicates) is too vague for you to understand, ask to be guided to resources that can help you interpret the symbols.

Like anything, accessing and using your Intuition in your business and daily life takes practice. You are learning a new language and like any new language, the integration into your vocabulary takes time. Be patient with yourself, and seek interpretation decoding in our free Facebook group **MAGIC NOT LOGIC with Julie & Tash Lewin**

INTUITIVE LANGUAGE WORKSHEETS

Signs & Signals Tracking Sheets for

Claircognizance
CLEAR KNOWING

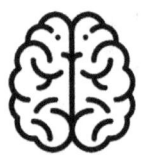

IDEAS POP INTO YOUR HEAD

What ideas came to you on a lightning bolt of inspiration?
Were they flashes or fully fledged ideas?

EXAMPLES:
Flashes of inspiration or ideas that come from nowhere.

What were you thinking about, contemplating or asking for guidance on when these occurred?

What revelations did you have when reflecting on the symbolism of these revelations? Were there other Senses involved?

SPONTANEOUS ACTIONS

What random or spontaneous actions have you taken lately, that upon reflection were incredibly well-timed?

EXAMPLES:
Taking spontaneous action without thought, only realising the impact on reflection.

What were you thinking about, contemplating or asking for guidance on when these occurred?

What revelations did you have when reflecting on the symbolism of these revelations?

INFORMATION DOWNLOADS

What information did you download and was it in a flash of insight or all of the information you required?

EXAMPLES:
Either getting flashes of insight or downloads of everything you need to know about a topic, person, event or place.

What were you thinking about, contemplating or asking for guidance on before these occurred?

What revelations did you have when reflecting on the symbolism of the information you downloaded?

INNER KNOWING

What experiences did you have of knowing something without knowing how you knew?

EXAMPLES:
You know where you are, even though you've never been there. You look at your phone seconds before it makes a sound. You think of someone, then you see them.

What were you thinking about, contemplating or asking for guidance on before/when these occurred?

What revelations did you have when reflecting on the meaning behind the information you knew?

IDEAS POP INTO YOUR HEAD

What ideas came to you on a lightning bolt of inspiration?
Were they flashes or fully fledged ideas?

EXAMPLES:
Flashes of inspiration or ideas that come from nowhere.

What were you thinking about, contemplating or asking for guidance on when these occurred?

What revelations did you have when reflecting on the symbolism of these revelations? Were there other Senses involved?

SPONTANEOUS ACTIONS

What random or spontaneous actions have you taken lately, that upon reflection were incredibly well-timed?

EXAMPLES:
Taking spontaneous action without thought, only realising the impact on reflection.

What were you thinking about, contemplating or asking for guidance on when these occurred?

What revelations did you have when reflecting on the symbolism of these revelations?

INFORMATION DOWNLOADS

What information did you download and was it in a flash of insight or all of the information you required?

EXAMPLES:
Either getting flashes of insight or downloads of everything you need to know about a topic, person, event or place.

What were you thinking about, contemplating or asking for guidance on before these occurred?

What revelations did you have when reflecting on the symbolism of the information you downloaded?

INNER KNOWING

What experiences did you have of knowing something without knowing how you knew?

EXAMPLES:
You know where you are, even though you've never been there. You look at your phone seconds before it makes a sound. You think of someone, then you see them.

What were you thinking about, contemplating or asking for guidance on before/when these occurred?

What revelations did you have when reflecting on the meaning behind the information you knew?

IDEAS POP INTO YOUR HEAD

What ideas came to you on a lightning bolt of inspiration?
Were they flashes or fully fledged ideas?

EXAMPLES:
Flashes of inspiration
or ideas that come
from nowhere.

What were you thinking about, contemplating or asking for
guidance on when these occurred?

What revelations did you have when reflecting on the symbolism
of these revelations? Were there other Senses involved?

SPONTANEOUS ACTIONS

What random or spontaneous actions have you taken lately, that upon reflection were incredibly well-timed?

EXAMPLES:
Taking spontaneous action without thought, only realising the impact on reflection.

What were you thinking about, contemplating or asking for guidance on when these occurred?

What revelations did you have when reflecting on the symbolism of these revelations?

INFORMATION DOWNLOADS

What information did you download and was it in a flash of insight or all of the information you required?

EXAMPLES:
Either getting flashes of insight or downloads of everything you need to know about a topic, person, event or place.

What were you thinking about, contemplating or asking for guidance on before these occurred?

What revelations did you have when reflecting on the symbolism of the information you downloaded?

INNER KNOWING

What experiences did you have of knowing something without knowing how you knew?

EXAMPLES:
You know where you are, even though you've never been there. You look at your phone seconds before it makes a sound. You think of someone, then you see them.

What were you thinking about, contemplating or asking for guidance on before/when these occurred?

What revelations did you have when reflecting on the meaning behind the information you knew?

IDEAS POP INTO YOUR HEAD

What ideas came to you on a lightning bolt of inspiration?
Were they flashes or fully fledged ideas?

EXAMPLES:
Flashes of inspiration or ideas that come from nowhere.

What were you thinking about, contemplating or asking for guidance on when these occurred?

What revelations did you have when reflecting on the symbolism of these revelations? Were there other Senses involved?

SPONTANEOUS ACTIONS

What random or spontaneous actions have you taken lately, that upon reflection were incredibly well-timed?

EXAMPLES:
Taking spontaneous action without thought, only realising the impact on reflection.

What were you thinking about, contemplating or asking for guidance on when these occurred?

What revelations did you have when reflecting on the symbolism of these revelations?

INFORMATION DOWNLOADS

What information did you download and was it in a flash of
insight or all of the information you required?

EXAMPLES:
Either getting
flashes of insight
or downloads of
everything you need
to know about a
topic, person, event
or place.

What were you thinking about, contemplating or asking for
guidance on before these occurred?

What revelations did you have when reflecting on the
symbolism of the information you downloaded?

INNER KNOWING

What experiences did you have of knowing something without knowing how you knew?

EXAMPLES:
You know where you are, even though you've never been there. You look at your phone seconds before it makes a sound. You think of someone, then you see them.

What were you thinking about, contemplating or asking for guidance on before/when these occurred?

What revelations did you have when reflecting on the meaning behind the information you knew?

IDEAS POP INTO YOUR HEAD

What ideas came to you on a lightning bolt of inspiration?
Were they flashes or fully fledged ideas?

EXAMPLES:
Flashes of inspiration or ideas that come from nowhere.

What were you thinking about, contemplating or asking for guidance on when these occurred?

What revelations did you have when reflecting on the symbolism of these revelations? Were there other Senses involved?

SPONTANEOUS ACTIONS

What random or spontaneous actions have you taken lately, that upon reflection were incredibly well-timed?

EXAMPLES:
Taking spontaneous action without thought, only realising the impact on reflection.

What were you thinking about, contemplating or asking for guidance on when these occurred?

What revelations did you have when reflecting on the symbolism of these revelations?

INFORMATION DOWNLOADS

What information did you download and was it in a flash of insight or all of the information you required?

EXAMPLES:
Either getting flashes of insight or downloads of everything you need to know about a topic, person, event or place.

What were you thinking about, contemplating or asking for guidance on before these occurred?

What revelations did you have when reflecting on the symbolism of the information you downloaded?

INNER KNOWING

What experiences did you have of knowing something without knowing how you knew?

EXAMPLES:
You know where you are, even though you've never been there. You look at your phone seconds before it makes a sound. You think of someone, then you see them.

What were you thinking about, contemplating or asking for guidance on before/when these occurred?

What revelations did you have when reflecting on the meaning behind the information you knew?

IDEAS POP INTO YOUR HEAD

What ideas came to you on a lightning bolt of inspiration?
Were they flashes or fully fledged ideas?

EXAMPLES:
Flashes of inspiration
or ideas that come
from nowhere.

What were you thinking about, contemplating or asking for
guidance on when these occurred?

What revelations did you have when reflecting on the symbolism
of these revelations? Were there other Senses involved?

SPONTANEOUS ACTIONS

What random or spontaneous actions have you taken lately, that upon reflection were incredibly well-timed?

EXAMPLES:
Taking spontaneous action without thought, only realising the impact on reflection.

What were you thinking about, contemplating or asking for guidance on when these occurred?

What revelations did you have when reflecting on the symbolism of these revelations?

INFORMATION DOWNLOADS

What information did you download and was it in a flash of
insight or all of the information you required?

EXAMPLES:
Either getting
flashes of insight
or downloads of
everything you need
to know about a
topic, person, event
or place.

What were you thinking about, contemplating or asking for
guidance on before these occurred?

What revelations did you have when reflecting on the
symbolism of the information you downloaded?

INNER KNOWING

What experiences did you have of knowing something without knowing how you knew?

EXAMPLES:
You know where you are, even though you've never been there. You look at your phone seconds before it makes a sound. You think of someone, then you see them.

What were you thinking about, contemplating or asking for guidance on before/when these occurred?

What revelations did you have when reflecting on the meaning behind the information you knew?

IDEAS POP INTO YOUR HEAD

What ideas came to you on a lightning bolt of inspiration?
Were they flashes or fully fledged ideas?

EXAMPLES:
Flashes of inspiration or ideas that come from nowhere.

What were you thinking about, contemplating or asking for guidance on when these occurred?

What revelations did you have when reflecting on the symbolism of these revelations? Were there other Senses involved?

SPONTANEOUS ACTIONS

What random or spontaneous actions have you taken lately, that upon reflection were incredibly well-timed?

EXAMPLES:
Taking spontaneous action without thought, only realising the impact on reflection.

What were you thinking about, contemplating or asking for guidance on when these occurred?

What revelations did you have when reflecting on the symbolism of these revelations?

INFORMATION DOWNLOADS

What information did you download and was it in a flash of insight or all of the information you required?

EXAMPLES:
Either getting flashes of insight or downloads of everything you need to know about a topic, person, event or place.

What were you thinking about, contemplating or asking for guidance on before these occurred?

What revelations did you have when reflecting on the symbolism of the information you downloaded?

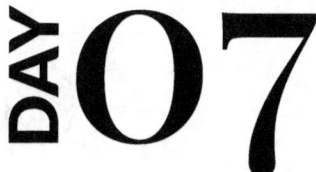

INNER KNOWING

What experiences did you have of knowing something without knowing how you knew?

EXAMPLES:
You know where you are, even though you've never been there. You look at your phone seconds before it makes a sound. You think of someone, then you see them.

What were you thinking about, contemplating or asking for guidance on before/when these occurred?

What revelations did you have when reflecting on the meaning behind the information you knew?

REFLECTION TIME

What did you discover about your Dominant Intuitive Language?

What signs & signals did you experience most often?

Did you access any of the other Dominant Intuitive Languages?

ACTIVITIES TO ENHANCE YOUR CONNECTION

When doing any tasks or activities where you are connecting with your Intuition, ask yourself: "What do I just know? Or what downloads am I getting?"

USING ORACLE/TAROT/ANGEL CARDS
1. Get your favourite deck of cards
2. Avoid using the guidebook that usually comes with them
3. Knock on the cards 3 times, as this clears residual energy
4. Ask a question, and shuffle the deck
5. Pull as many cards as you feel called to pull; you may pull the card on top or you can wait for one to fly out of the deck as you are shuffling
6. Lay the cards out in front of you
7. Close your eyes, take 3 deep breaths & connect in to your Spirit Team. Ask them to put a gold white light of protection around you, to raise your vibration to it's highest frequency. This will ensure that you only access wisdom from high frequency beings.
8. Look at each card individually, and then all of them as a whole. You will be using both the symbolism on the cards and also whatever downloads you receive to tell a story. You will be creating a metaphor during this stage
9. Journal what you discover during this experience. This will help you decode the metaphor. Allow any other experiences or Senses to come into play at this time. Write about it all
10. Remember, you are an open channel and you will just know. Trust that you know, and don't second guess what comes to mind

FIND YOUR WAY HOME
1. Go to an unfamiliar place
2. Find your way home without using maps
3. Journal your experience *"what happened along the way?"*, *"was it easy or did you find it difficult"*, *"did you use any of the other Senses"*, *"Did you make it home without maps?"*

COOK WITHOUT A RECIPE
1. Find a meal you have never cooked before but you have eaten
2. Identify the ingredients by tasting, looking, feeling and smelling the meal
3. Create your own recipe based on the ingredients and the steps your Intuition tells you will be required
4. Cook the meal, and see how close you came
5. Decode the knowledge downloads you received while doing this exercise, and journal your experience

SIGNS & SIGNALS TALLY SHEET

TIME	DATE	SIGN TYPE	DESCRIPTION	LOCATION
9:04am	12.06.2020	Smell	Dry dog food	At office desk

SIGNS & SIGNALS TALLY SHEET

TIME	DATE	SIGN TYPE	DESCRIPTION	LOCATION

SIGNS & SIGNALS TALLY SHEET

TIME	DATE	SIGN TYPE	DESCRIPTION	LOCATION

SIGNS & SIGNALS TALLY SHEET

TIME	DATE	SIGN TYPE	DESCRIPTION	LOCATION

SIGNS & SIGNALS TALLY SHEET

TIME	DATE	SIGN TYPE	DESCRIPTION	LOCATION

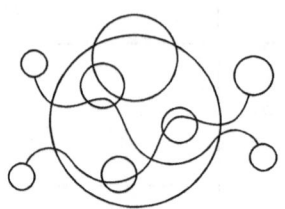

Lightcode Lab™

CLEARING & ACTIVATION CODES
FOR ENTREPRENEURIAL SUCCESS

JULIE & TASH LEWIN
Mother-Daughter Duo
lightcodelab.com
@lightcodelab
support@lightcodelab.com

www.ingramcontent.com/pod-product-compliance
Lightning Source LLC
Chambersburg PA
CBHW071917290426
44110CB00013B/1389